Hebraic Learning
את

We (as Hebrew parents) are to look at our children, face to face and verbally tell them the history of our ancestor's freedom from slavery! Feel confident and free, to use this book as your family's Haggadah, and tell our history in a play-like, fun and entertaining way, for the entire family!!!

Son:

Excuse me Dad,
why do we celebrate
the Feast of Passover?

Father:

Well son,

grab the Scriptures and
let's turn to Exodus 13.

Passover:
Pesach פסח

Telling Our Story

Author & Main Illustrator:
Keyz Kreations & Kingdom Khai

Co. Illustrator:
Broderick Barnes
כבדיה

Hebraic Learning
את

The Haggadah (Hebrew: הַגָּדָה‎ ,"telling"; plural: Haggadot) is a text that sets forth the order of the Passover Seder. Reading the Haggadah at the Seder table is a way of honoring the mitzvah (command) for each Hebrew to "tell your son" of the story from the Book of Exodus. It is all about the Hebrews being delivered from slavery in Egypt by the hand of Yah. ("And thou shalt tell thy son in that day, saying: It is because of that which Yah did for me when I came forth out of Egypt." Ex. 13:8).

Haggadah comes from the Hebrew word Nagad.

נגד (n.g.d/nagad) Translation:
BE.FACE.TO.FACE (V) Definition: To face another. KJV Translations: tell, declare, show, utter, expound, messenger, report, issue Strong's Hebrew #: h.5046

Scriptures

Exodus 13:8-10

On that day you are to tell your son, 'It is because of what Yah did for me when I left Egypt.'

9 "Moreover, it will serve you as a sign on your hand and as a reminder between your eyes, so that Yah's Torah may be on your lips; because with a strong hand Yah brought you out of Egypt. 10 Therefore you are to observe this regulation at its proper time, year after year.

Scriptures

Narrator:

Long ago, in the land of Egypt, a group of people called the Hebrews served for the Pharoah, the king of Egypt.

The Pharoah oppressed the Hebrew people but he did not know that these were to be the chosen people of Yah, the Creator of all things. When the people cried out for freedom from their oppression, The Creator heard them. He sent a Hebrew shepherd named Moses to free His people.

Narrator:

Moses was a Hebrew that was raised as an Egyptian in Pharaoh's house. He later fled to Midian after killing an Egyptian for beating a Hebrew. 40 years later Yah called Moses to save His people.

Israel
Midian
Egypt

Narrator:

Yah's servant, Moses, and Moses' brother Aaron, were told to speak to the Pharoah and tell him to let the people go. Pharoah refused and 9 plagues came upon Egypt. The tenth was going to be the worst. This is the story of Passover and the freedom of the people of Yah.

Moses: *Ex.12:21-23*

Then Moses called all of the elders of Israel together and said to them: "Go at once and select the animals for your families and slaughter the Passover lamb. 22 Take a bunch of hyssop, dip it into the blood in the basin and put some of the blood on the top and on both sides of the doorframe. None of you shall go out of the door of your house until morning. 23 When Yah goes through the land to strike down the Egyptians, He will see the blood on the top and sides of the doorframe and will pass over that doorway, and He will not permit the destroyer to enter your houses and strike you down. And ye shall observe this thing for an ordinance to thee and to thy sons for ever.

Moses: *Ex.12:25-27*
"When you come to the land which Yah will give you, as he has promised, you are to observe this ceremony. 26 When your children ask you, 'What do you mean by this ceremony?' 27 say, 'It is the sacrifice of Yah's Pesach [Passover], because [Yah] passed over the houses of the people of Isra'el in Egypt, when he killed the Egyptians but spared our houses.'" The people of Isra'el bowed their heads and worshipped.

Narrator:

And all the people gathered their animals and did as Moses had said.

Narrator:

This was a sign that the Hebrew people rejected Pharaoh and the deities of Egypt and were choosing to serve Yah.

Narrator:

When midnight struck, the destroyer came and slaughtered all the firstborn of Egypt. But it passed over the houses of Israel because on the doorpost was the blood of the lamb.

Narrator:

The very next day, the Hebrews left Egypt in haste. They were freed from slavery by the Hand of Yah!

Narrator:
As they traveled, they came to the Red Sea. How would they get across?

Narrator:
Pharaoh and his army regretted letting the people go and chased behind them to get them back.

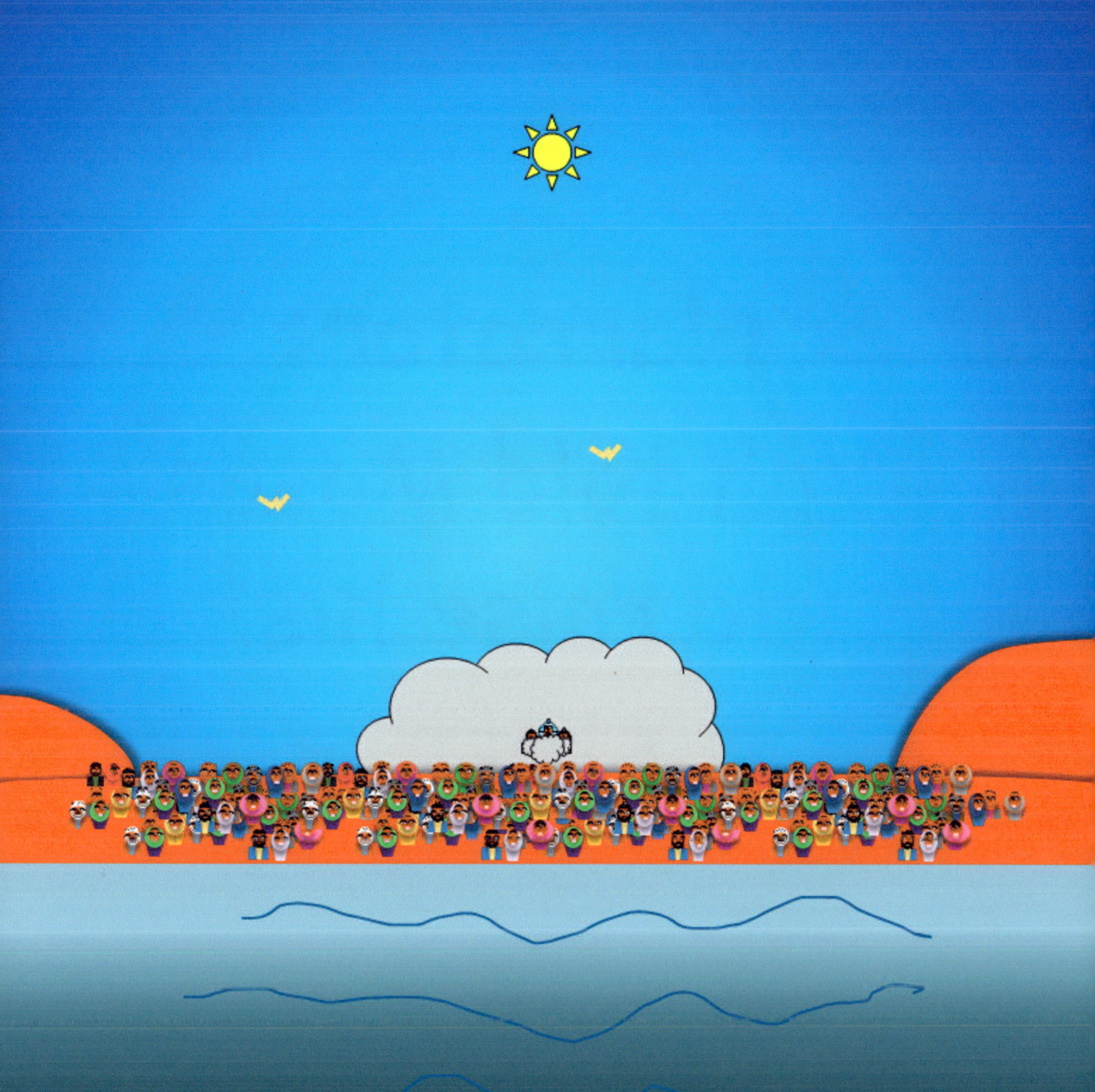

Narrator:
Yah told Moses
to raise his
staff.

Narrator:
And when he did, the water parted...

Narrator:
...and the Hebrews walked through the Red Sea on dry land.

Narrator:
But Pharoah's
army followed
them...

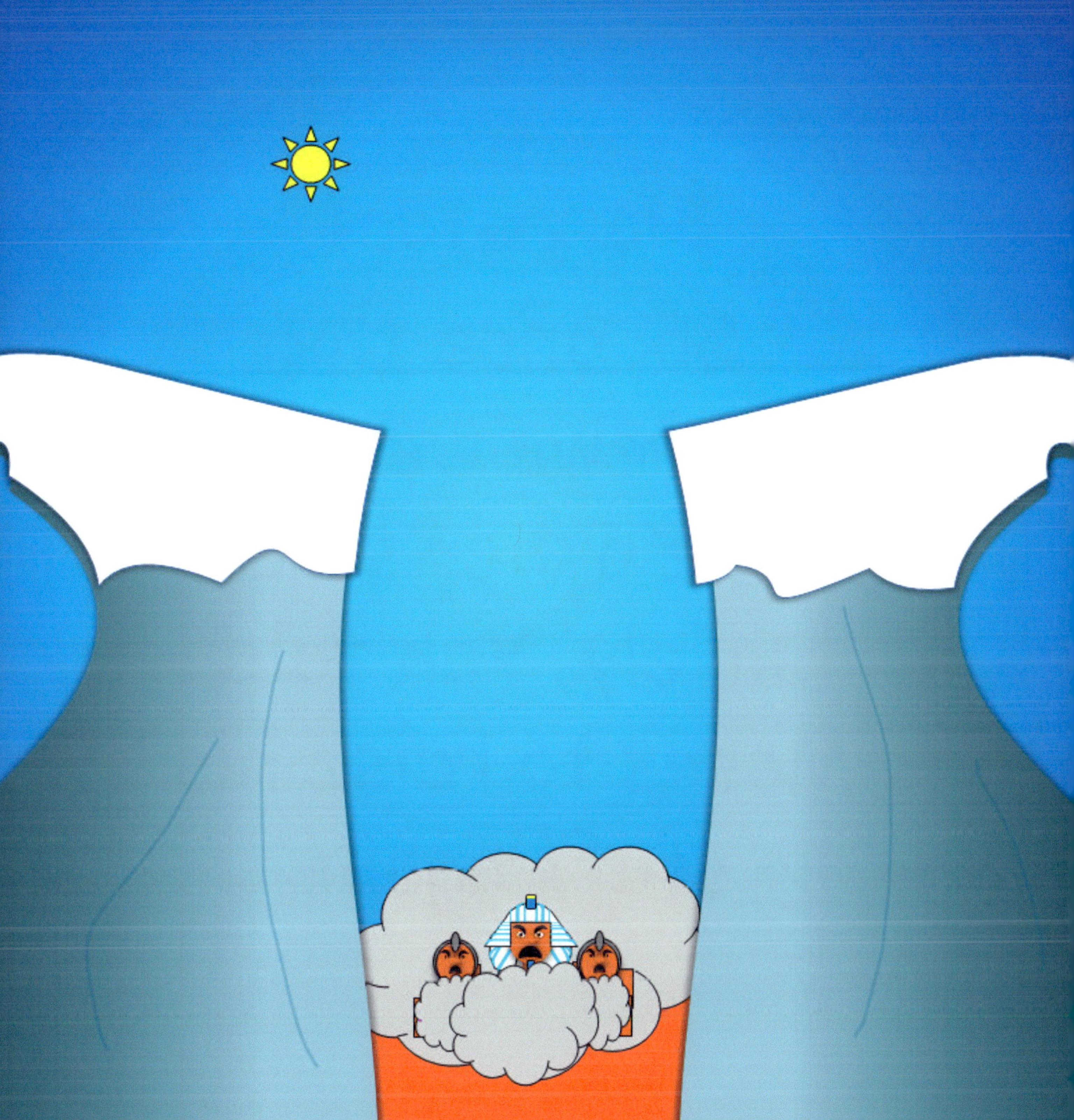

Narrator:
So, once the Hebrews were on the other side safely, Yah told Moses to raise his staff again.

Narrator:
All the water came crashing down back to its place, the Egyptian army was destroyed, not one survived.

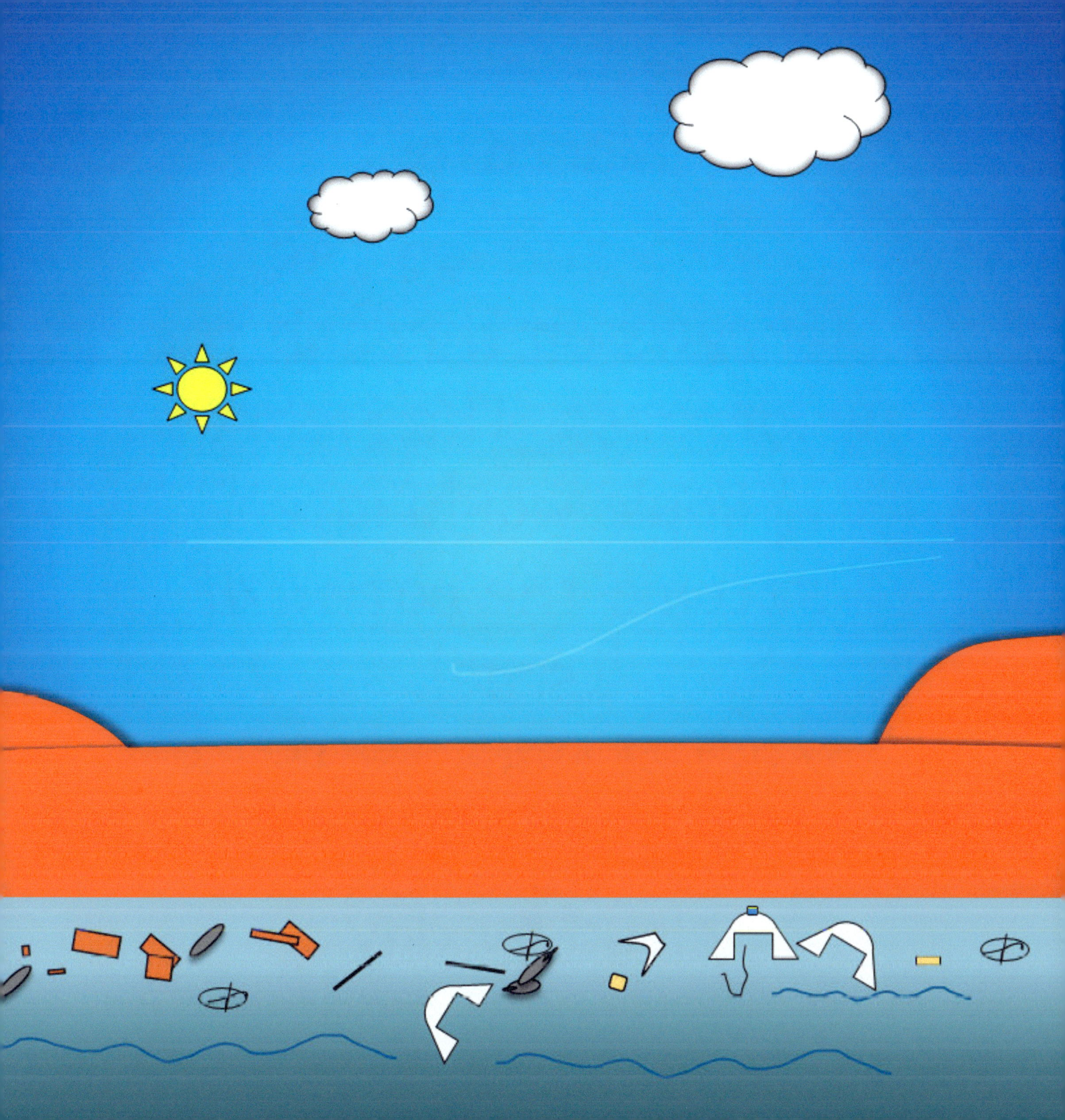

Narrator:

And Yah led the Hebrews on through the wilderness. The Hebrew people would later become the nation of Israel.

Yah led them on their way using a pillar of cloud by day...

Narrator:
...and He used a pillar of fire to lead them by night.

Father:
And that is the Story of Passover. It's Our Story. The Story of Yah leading our people to freedom. This is why we celebrate the Passover. And when you have children, it's your job to tell them Our Story.

To Be Continued...
for Shavuot!

The

End

If you enjoyed this book, be sure to check out our other books!

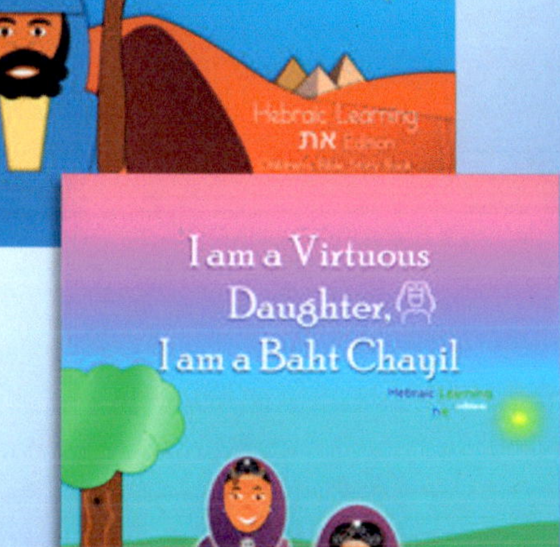

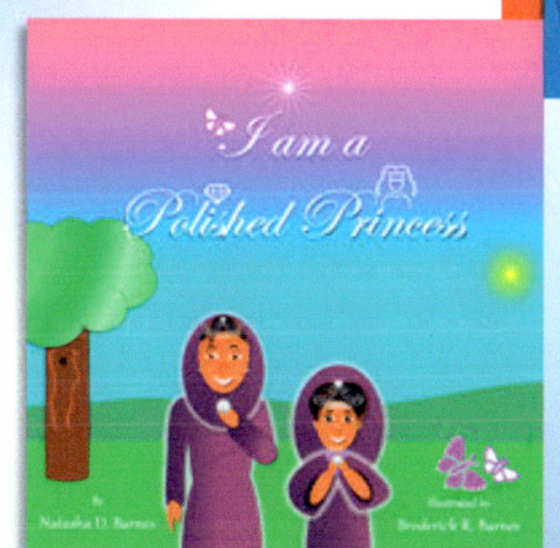

...and be on the lookout for the next book in the "We Are Lights" Children's book series!

www.KingdomKhai.com

Kingdom Khai

Cultivating World Class Kingdom Resources

Made in the USA
Monee, IL
07 July 2026

56550085R00031